The SUNFLOWERS

Vincent van Gogh's Search for Beauty

Zahra Marwan

Feiwel and Friends
New York

In a small room in an even smaller apartment,
Vincent van Gogh made paintings.

He lived in Paris, which was gray and blue, busy and refined.

The paintings weren't sophisticated by any means. And most people found them to be inelegant.

The grays and browns and blues of old shoes
that matched the elegantly grimy city.

It was his paintings of sunflowers
that he loved more than anything.

And if sunflowers were considered inelegant, Vincent loved them anyway. He listened closely to his heart.

He went to local coffee shops to see
and hear what other artists thought.

There, he met a new friend, Paul Gauguin.

Paul painted faraway places that were brighter and more vibrant than anything Vincent had ever seen. People in heavy coats and hats were replaced with those in floral prints. Vincent thought they were simply wonderful.

Vincent shared his beloved sunflower paintings
with Paul. And Paul loved them.

Bleu

Bleu

Bleu 4 Bleu + 0 jaune = Bleu

3 " + 1 " = bleujaune

2 " + 2 " = jaune

1 " + 3 " = vertjaune

Jaune 0 " + 4 " = jaune

Jaune

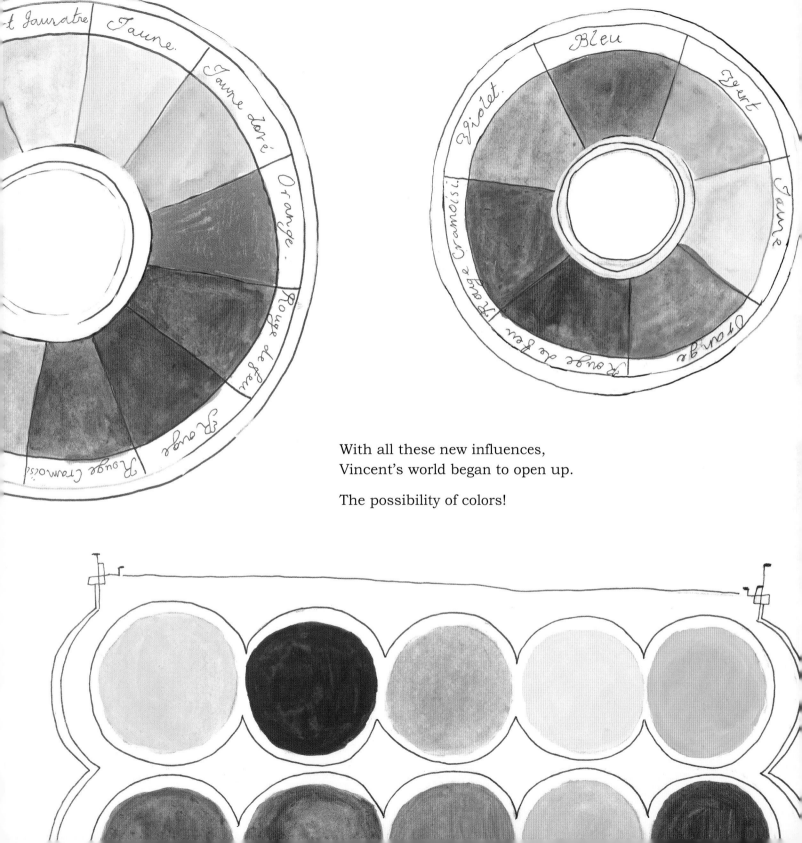

With all these new influences,
Vincent's world began to open up.

The possibility of colors!

And with the help of his younger brother Theo,
Vincent decided to travel and find inspiration
in more colorful places.

He packed up his art supplies and a few
belongings and left Paris through sunflower
fields and villages to a small city called Arles.

He quickly moved into a yellow house, where he set up a table to write his letters to Theo, feeling very eager for Paul, who was to join him.

Vincent had never felt better than he did in his new city. With every person he met, his paintings became brighter and more colorful. He painted and painted!

Wheat, the night sky, and the sea.
He was so happy, he even painted
the almond as it blossomed.

He had never created this many paintings in his life.
No more paintings made of dark grays and browns—
everything was alive with color now.

But something was still missing.

It wasn't too long before he
received a package from Paul.
A mailed painted portrait of
Paul. Vincent sent him a
self-portrait back.

His friend would soon arrive with more canvas for them both, and they would cut it together. Until then, Vincent was alone.

He listened closely to his troubled heart.

Vincent wanted to create
meaning. He wanted to paint
with thought and emotion,
and not only what he saw.

He used intense colors to express his feelings. It was like speaking poetry just by arranging colors, like hearing comforting things in music.

He made more inelegant sunflower paintings, which were richer and more beautiful than ever. These sunflowers gave Vincent meaning.

These will comfort people with troubled hearts, he thought.

They comforted his troubled heart.

He painted sunflower after sunflower, a few of them to decorate his friend's room. Some paintings he loved so much, he made them twice. The exact same painting, twice. One for himself, and the other for Paul.

Bright and inelegant, yellow on yellow and yellow on blue. He didn't always arrange the sunflowers neatly in a vase, but separately on a table.

For now, he was alone, before his guest
would arrive. But many people were on his
mind. He wrote letters to his brother Theo,
saying, *I missed you the first few days,
and it was strange for me not to find you
when I came home in the afternoon.*

And Theo wrote back that he loved Vincent's new paintings. That Paul did too, and that he was on his way to see him.

The yellow house was ready with paintings of wheat fields against hills as large as the sea. Delicate pale greens, the flowering of a potato plant. The sea was not just blue, but made of many other colors.

Vincent changed the way colors do.
Vibrant and full of feeling, he was
prepared to welcome his dear friend.

Vincent's heart could hardly contain his joy
and anticipation, just like his color box, which
could hardly contain all his paints.

When Paul arrived, he looked at
the sunflower paintings that hung
in his room at the yellow house.
He loved them so much.

He could feel how powerful and full of meaning
the sunflower paintings were.

He could feel the way it is to have a real friend.

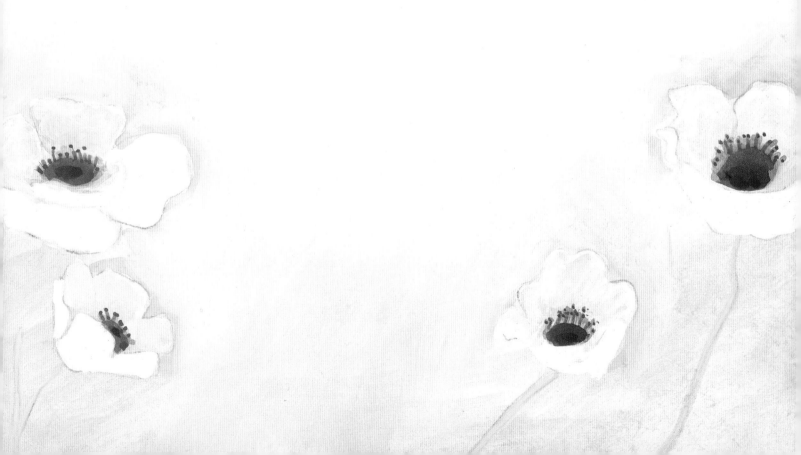

Author's Note

The French word for sunflower is "tournesol," which means "turns with the sun." It wasn't until much later in his life that Vincent van Gogh found his direction.

Like so many of us, Vincent had no idea what he wanted to do or be. He tried to be an art dealer, a bookseller, a priest, a teacher, and, finally, a painter. He was always thinking and feeling and wondering. Sometimes he felt really sad, but he was determined to find beauty. It seems he also followed the direction of the sun.

Vincent made paintings of flowers and people and objects the way many other artists did at the time. But painting sunflowers was unique. Vincent saw qualities in sunflowers that other people may have overlooked. While other artists considered sunflowers to be coarse and unrefined, he found beauty in them. His paintings of sunflowers were so special that people began to think of him when seeing sunflowers, just as he had hoped. They became so closely related to him that his friends even brought sunflowers to his funeral.

The way Vincent was inspired to create sunflower paintings to decorate his friend's room before his arrival really moved me. It reminded me of how much love we have for one another. We think of each other. We sometimes prepare a space in anticipation of one another. I have made many drawings and compositions of my friends. Most of my artwork is based on very personal stories of people I know or love.

I have made a drawing of listening to my friend read an endearing letter that his grandfather left him. Of visiting my friend in his former art space the Rose Studio to see his paintings, make jokes, and share advice with each other. I've made a drawing of walking to a Roman aqueduct behind my friend's home in France, where figs fall into the water. Or, within that same beautiful friendship, going to see art or the sea together when I felt homesick. I even made a painting of a friend who played the banjo for me under a Paris willow tree before leaving to go back to Seattle.

I've made so many drawings of friends who have warmly welcomed me in their lives, their homes, and their families, filling my life with so much beauty and color. The beauty of art and friendship is a way for all of us to comfort our troubled hearts.

To all the friends I've ever loved

A Feiwel and Friends Book
An imprint of Macmillan Publishing Group, LLC
120 Broadway, New York, NY 10271 • mackids.com

Our books may be purchased in bulk for promotional, educational, or
business use. Please contact your local bookseller or the Macmillan Corporate
and Premium Sales Department at (800) 221-7945 ext. 5442 or by email
at MacmillanSpecialMarkets@macmillan.com.

Library of Congress Control Number: 2023948969

First edition, 2024
Book design by Mike Burroughs

Created with watercolor and ink, pens and pencils, light paper to
sketch on, and watercolor paper or tinted board for the finished art.

Feiwel and Friends logo designed by Filomena Tuosto
Printed in China by Toppan Leefung Printing Ltd., Dongguan City, Guangdong Province

ISBN 978-1-250-85963-1
1 3 5 7 9 10 8 6 4 2